SINGLE
AND
SATISFIED

A CLOSE LOOK AT LOVE, SEX AND RELATIONSHIPS

LLOYD ALLEN

authorHOUSE®

AuthorHouse™
1663 Liberty Drive
Bloomington, IN 47403
www.authorhouse.com
Phone: 1 (800) 839-8640

Published by AuthorHouse   11/09/2016

ISBN: 978-1-5246-2053-0 (sc)
ISBN: 978-1-5246-2052-3 (e)

KJV
Scripture quotations marked KJV are from the Holy Bible, King James Version (Authorized Version). First published in 1611. Quoted from the KJV Classic Reference Bible, Copyright © 1983 by The Zondervan Corporation.

CONTENTS

This book is dedicated with deep love and
appreciation to my loving family:
My wife and sweetheart, Rae Christine Allen,
and our two sons, Lloyd (Jr.) and Daniel.
Their love, patience, understanding,
and encouragement
have been my source of inspiration.

ACKNOWLEDGMENTS

I am deeply grateful—
To my parents and in-laws, Edgar, Lucille,
Rodolfo, and Vilma, for teaching my wife
and me important lessons in life.

To my loving wife and sweetheart, Rae Christine, for
exemplifying Christian virtues that distinguish her
as the woman any man could dream of marrying.
I thank her for patiently and lovingly
traversing this journey
with me in developing this book.

To our two children, Lloyd (Jr.) and Daniel,
for their love, patience, and understanding
as they loaned me to the manuscript.

To my church family at the Cooper City SDA
Church for their inspiration and encouragement to
forge ahead in writing and publishing this book.

To my Father in heaven, who has given me great
lessons on singleness, through the medium of His
word and my personal experiences, and the wisdom
and inspiration to translate these lessons into words.

INTRODUCTION

This book is my heart poured out. To witness people passing through life from day to day by a method of trial and error, surrendering a confident and meaningful existence to chance and happenstance, breaks my heart.

I was not endowed with the luxury of being born in a Christian family. My parents, particularly my mother, were ardent believers in formal education, so I, along with my siblings, was compelled to attend school without negotiation. But attending academic institutions was inadequate to equip me with a true sense of identity and purpose.

It was God's call on my life when I was introduced to, and subsequently baptized into, the church at a tender age. At this juncture of my life, my sail was positioned as I began learning the fundamental secret of successful living. The underlying secret is that I was created and fashioned by a Supreme Manufacturer, who has furnished me with explicit instruction regarding my proper maintenance and upkeep (just like the designing of a motorcar). If I deviated from, or failed to strictly adhere to, the instructions clearly delineated in His instruction manual, my heart would ache and my soul suffer—my life a chaotic mess and my existence marked by painful regret and purposelessness. But conversely, if I set my heart to seek out His ways and my life to conform to his wise counsel, then my heart would know no boundary in the enjoyment of peace. My happiness would be measureless, and my life would be a paragon of purpose and meaning.

My hope is that

1. every youth will find in these pages a clear-cut, direct, and unequivocal set of instructions that will serve as a road map to lead him or her triumphantly into adulthood;

2. every single who is searching for love and relationship will find practical and insightful guidelines that will steer him or her into the arms of the one who will fulfill their lifelong dream for intimate joy and satisfaction;

3. the singles who have opted for a life of chastity and abstinence will secure an enlightened understanding of God's will for their lives and their place in his plan, and how they can maximize the advantages of their single state to lead a life of effectiveness and satisfaction; and

4. every mother, father, mentor, coach, and caregiver will find invaluable information and time-tested truth to assist them in successfully guiding the feet of those committed to their charge.

TAP INTO YOUR FULL POTENTIAL.

God has made us a little lower than the angels, has crowned us with glory and honor, and has appointed us stewards over the works of His hands (Hebrews 2:7). We are distinguished from, and placed in a superior position to the animals because of our endowment with a brain to think, explore, invent, and be creative. Recognizing this superior position of intelligence and wisdom, God charged Adam, the first man, with the responsibility of managing the domain of his immediate surroundings (Genesis 1:28). Every person has a divine duty to engage in the work of strengthening and developing his mental faculties.

Ellen G. White, one of my favorite authors, couched these sentiments in sublime language when she advises that God is displeased when we do not seek the highest development of our intellectual powers.

TRAIN AND DISCIPLINE THE MIND—No matter who you are ... the Lord has blessed you with intellectual faculties capable of vast improvement. Cultivate your talents with persevering earnestness. Train and discipline the mind by study, by observation, by reflection. You cannot meet the mind of God unless you put to use every power. The mental faculties will strengthen and develop if you will go to work in the fear of God, in humility, and with earnest prayer. A resolute purpose will accomplish wonders. (Ellen G. White, *Life Sketches of Ellen G. White*, 275)

HAVE YOU BEEN OFFENDED? CULTIVATE A KIND AND FORGIVING SPIRIT.

"Moreover if thy brother shall trespass against thee, go and tell him his fault between thee and him alone: if he shall hear thee, thou hast gained thy brother" (Matthew 18:15).

Don't be harsh.

Remember your own state, that you are as feeble and fickle as clay. You are not infallible. Instead you are as prone to mistakes as anyone else. If for one moment the unregenerate impulse of your own heart excites you to be insensitive or harsh with the offender, then you risk having the same stern rebuke leveled at you as the accusers in Jesus's time. "Let him that is without sin cast the first stone." These were the words spoken by Jesus to the vile accusers that mercilessly dragged the woman caught in adultery to the feet of Jesus. How the Discerner of souls afforded men an opportunity to search their own souls. Struck with a sense of conviction and guilt, they quietly excused themselves from the presence of Him who read the barbarism of their own hearts.

Be kind. Be gentle. Be magnanimous.

Everyone at some point in his or her life needs the understanding, the mercy, yea the silence of another. Place yourself in the other person's shoe. You too have been down in the gutters. You too have cried desperately to the Father, "Let this cup pass from me." Then be large-hearted and great-souled in your treatment of others. Never jump to conclusions. Never make assumptions, for many times they are false assumptions. Give the offender an opportunity to express, explain, and discuss his side of the story. You may just be surprised to learn that the person was well-intentioned, free from any malicious motive. In the end, you will be pleased that you have saved a soul from hell.

BROKEN PROMISES AND SHATTERED DREAMS

"Call unto me, and I will answer thee, and shew thee great and mighty things, which thou knowest not" (Jeremiah 33:3).

You have been hurt by a wife, husband, child, parent, or friend. The more you rehearse the details of the seemingly senseless and insensitive act, the deeper the roots of bitterness and grief permeate the tender lining of your aching heart. The lion within you wants to destroy. Like the unrighteous witch of Endor, you massage your soul with cruel and diabolic deliberations. "O how I wish my offender could be as though they never existed." You vow that you will not just get mad, but get even.

The heart throbs, the blood surges through the veins, the eyes bulge, and the chest tightens. You have reached the boiling point. Your usefulness is compromised, your thoughts of progress are crippled, and evil is doing its perfect work.

Apply the brakes, friend. Refuse to be thrown over the edge by the destroyer of souls. There's a prayer you can utter. There's a God who can help: My God, my King, and my Creator. Consider my frame. Remember that I am dust. You made me and you can re-create me. Please come nigh unto me and help. Remove from me this pain that is chiseling through my soul. I need you, and only you, to come and anoint my bruised heart. Loving Father, Great Physician, come and perform a mighty work. I lay contrite and broken on your surgical table. Take the double-edged knife of the Holy Spirit and cut and scrape and remove every cancerous tissue that would metastasize to destroy the good seeds you have planted in me. Then gentle Savior, apply the liniment of your love, your sweet spirit to heal and refresh me. Help me to live again. Restore to me the joy of thy salvation, and make me wholly thine. Help my offender. Help his soul. Make him thine. I thank you for your matchless power to heal and restore. I praise your holy name. In Jesus's name.

Free yourself of resentment and vindictiveness. Remember, when you forgive, you just released a prisoner, and that prisoner was yourself.

THE LIE OF CASUAL SEX

Sex: A Neurological Understanding

It is time we raised an alarm and cried from the top of our lungs that people should cease committing silent suicide by engaging in casual sex. It is a lie that "everybody is doing it," so it's okay. It is a lie that it is inconsequential to hook up with a stranger—that there is no potential danger. It is a lie that you are just having a good time, "enjoying the party," and there are no possible repercussions after the bells are hushed and the lights are dimmed. Some people are lying to you. This sex-craze culture is lying to you. The hormones surging throughout your body are sending you messages that you are misinterpreting, and you are leading a life that will bring you heartache, misery, and painful regret.

The Section of Your Brain that Transmits Messages that You Are Likely to Misinterpret

This section of the brain that sends emotion-charged messages is called the amygdala, located at the rear of the brain. The section of the brain that controls reason and proper judgment is called the prefrontal cortex of the brain's frontal lobe. According to scientific research this section of the brain does not mature until a person grows out of adolescence and is well into their mid-twenties. While young people can make some good judgment calls for themselves, it is impossible for them to make fully mature judgment decisions until their midtwenties, when their brains are finally mature.1

Do you understand better why teenage marriages are not to be encouraged? A person not out of the teen years lacks, to a large extent, the insight and proper judgment to assess the fitness of one to whom he or she must commit to for the rest of his or her life. You cannot make proper decisions just relying on the electromagnetic messages of the amygdala, the section of the brain concerned with the emotion. Even the perception of another person's face is associated with an emotional response within the amygdala.2

How powerful are these messages? Decisions about sex must not be made just based on what the emotion judges as "good" or "feels good." Following these compelling emotional urges could lead a person into making decisions that could translate into a possible destruction of his or her own life.

Now don't be displeased with your Creator for designing an emotional center in your brain. He had good reasons for doing so, for in marriage and other areas of life, we need a measure of emotion to ensure a balanced existence.

How Sleeping around Negatively Impacts a Marriage

There is a bonding mechanism in the brain that is triggered when two people engage in sexual intercourse. The brain is comprised of billions of neurons. A neuron consists of a cell body containing the nucleus and the surrounding fluid called the cytoplasm. The neuron is the primary component of the brain. There is another cell called the synapse. The synapses bridge the gap between neurons, and are responsible for brain activities such as memory, desires, emotion, and behavior. These cells are sustained or are allowed to deteriorate based on how often the behaviors and activities are experienced.

When people engage in sex, the synapses light up and strengthen as they spread across the neurons. An attachment or bonding is created like a Band-Aid or adhesive tape. This initial bonding is very strong. When sex is engaged in with another partner, as when people sleep around, the bonding for the new partner is drastically weakened; just like the adhesive tape that loses its ability to bond when used a second or third time. The initial bonding mechanism has been damaged.

This is why people who have sexual relationships with multiple partners before marriage are more likely to divorce than people who were virgins when they got married.

Studies with young people who sleep around have consistently confirmed that the young people feel that the tearing away of the bonding mechanism in the brain has the left them feeling dirty, maltreated, and unwanted, and this sad aftermath of sexual immorality has even driven some to commit suicide.

Research shows that 3 percent of girls and 7 percent of boys are at risk of committing suicide as a result of a feeling of worthlessness from sexual immorality. It is interesting that science is just confirming what has been postulated by Divine wisdom hundreds of years ago: "Flee from sexual immorality. All other sins a person commits are outside the body, but whoever sins sexually, sins against their own body" (1 Corinthians 6:18, New International Version).

The Threat of STDs

This story was aired on one of Dr. James Dobson's radio programs. The young man, while at college, engaged in casual sex, believing it was inconsequential. He left college, got married, and was elated to see his firstborn, a bouncing baby girl. To his shocking discovery, he had passed on to his wife herpes, a sexually transmitted disease that he had contracted from a one-night stand while at college. The mother, in turn, passed on the disease to the fetus, and the child was born with severe health effects. Imagine for a moment the heartache, the emotional trauma, the painful regret experienced by this young man to see his innocent wife with a disease that she must battle for a long time; and a baby suffering from a disease she did not bargain for. All because of one mistake, one instance of yielding to the lie of a sex-crazed culture that eloquently preaches that sleeping around is okay, that casual sex is cool, and that sexual immorality is innocent fun.

Awake from your slumber, friends. Cease committing silent suicide. Protect your health, protect your body, protect your life; and guard jealously the health and well-being of those you love dearly.

DO YOU HAVE UNRESOLVED ISSUES,

"baggage," or "junk in your trunk" with which you need to deal?

Deal with *you* first, before you commence the process of dating. Take yourself off the market until you get your issues fixed. Consider this scenario. The young lady is married to the man of her dreams. A misunderstanding arises in the marriage, and they sit down to discuss it with the hope of clarifying their thoughts and arriving at an amicable conclusion. Then something happened that mystified the new kid on the marriage block. She quickly arose and left the room in a rage, slammed the door boisterously, and shouted, "I don't want to hear it. I'm done; it's over." From his standpoint, there was nothing he could pinpoint that triggered that sudden outburst. No abusive language was used, and one negative word was spoken. They were having a civil conversation, he insisted. He tried to converse with her, seeking earnestly a reason for that mysterious behavior. He was simply speechless.

For the next seven days, they lived in the same house and slept in the same bed, but she never uttered a word to him, even though he tried desperately to restore normalcy in their home life. The six-month-old marriage was nearing a breaking point. Bewildered and frustrated, he asked her, "Honey, are we going to lose our marriage because I spent thirty-five dollars from our joint account to purchase a pair of shoes without previously consulting you?"

"That's not it," she quipped.

"So what is it? Can you please tell me the reason?" He was passionate and sincere.

For the first time in more than a week, she decided to come to grips with, and reveal, the compelling motive for her behavior. She told him that she grew up in a home where her dad, who was extremely abusive to her mother, was a control freak. In addition to the physical and verbal abuse, he would also control her finances, dictating how she spent every penny. Experiencing a feeling of deep empathy for her mom, and anger and hatred toward her dad, she resolved that she would take stern action in her marriage if she felt dissatisfied with her husband's management of their finances. She vowed that the moment he spent a dime, even on food, without her prior knowledge, there would be pandemonium in the home, and she would be filing for divorce forthwith. She declared further that she hates men, and no man can ever be trusted, for all men are abusers.

Did you know that if a child has witnessed abuse in the home being inflicted by one parent toward the other, that child essentially has sustained abuse herself/himself?

If you have been abused sexually, emotionally, or verbally, or you have other past experiences that have negatively impacted your life, you should be healed by God first. You are not a fit candidate for a marriage relationship. Don't look for someone to fix or complete you. Get fixed before starting a relationship. As a child, you have been sexually or emotionally abused by a family member, friend, or stranger. You live with a relative who emotionally or verbally abused you, constantly putting you down, using disparaging or demeaning remarks to erode your self-esteem or to disgrace your humanity. You were told that you'll never amount to anything, and, like a self-fulfilling prophecy, you internalized those messages and forged a life of recklessness and purposelessness. You might have been in a relationship where you were the victim of domestic abuse, and you have become confused about your own identity. I implore you, friends. This is not the time to seek a romantic relationship. Rather it is time to seek healing of mind, body, and spirit. Getting involved in a relationship at this juncture of your life can only place you at risk of repeating the cycle of dysfunctionality. It's time to stop hell going and start heaven all over again. You must confront and bring closure to past hurt and emotional scars. You cannot afford to enter marriage with "baggage" that could mar the happiness of your newly established family. God releases you to marry only after he has dealt with your issues.

> It's time to stop hell going and
> start heaven all over again.
> You must confront and bring closure
> to past hurt and emotional scars.

DON'T BE INVOLVED
BEFORE YOU EVALUATE.

––––––––––––––

If they are not believers, then you should not date them.

Don't survey them. Don't try them. Don't scope them. Don't experiment with them.

You can't them the one. They are not the one. If they don't live up, they won't line up.

If you are a believer, and you are attracted to an unbeliever, then undoubtedly something is wrong with your profession of faith.

Evaluate. Engage in some checks and balances, and exercise care in whom you choose to invest your time. It's not difficult to be overcome by infatuation, and eventually fall in love and marry someone you don't really want.

Let's ponder this question recorded in the book of Amos: "Can two walk together, except they be agreed?" (Amos 3:3).

What does a believer have in common with an unbeliever?

The apostle Paul spoke with clarity in his exhortation to the believers.

Endowed with divine authority and inspiration he admonishes: Be ye not unequally yoked together with unbelievers: for what fellowship hath righteousness with unrighteousness and what communion hath light with darkness? (2 Corinthians 6:14–16).

If it is your plan to eventually marry and start a family, it is important that you remember that God places a high regard on marriage—the institution that is designed to birth the next generation, to provide future leaders of our society, and to prepare a people for citizenship in His kingdom. What solemn vows to make before God and the waiting universe, what contract of eternal significance to which to commit. It is a faithful saying that your happiness is sealed, and your destiny, to a large extent, is determined on the day you marry.

Abraham so understood the far-reaching implication and the eternal significance of marriage that he passionately appealed to his servant not to gamble with, or treat with scant regard, the important decision of finding a wife for his son. This compendium of wisdom and knowledge called the Bible records the earnest entreaty of a loving father (for a wife for Isaac). Abraham said to his servant, the oldest of his household, who had charge of all that he owned, "Please place your hand under my thigh, and I will make you swear by the LORD, the God of heaven and the God of earth, that you shall not take a wife for my son from the daughters of the Canaanites, among whom I live, but you will go to my country and to my relatives, and take a wife for my son Isaac" (Genesis 24:3, New American Standard Bible).

A DIFFERENT LIFESTYLE—The character and course of the Christian is in marked contrast to that of worldlings. The Christian cannot find pleasure in the amusements and in the varied scenes of gaiety of the world. Higher and holier attractions engage the affections. Christians will show that they are the friends of God by their obedience. "Ye are my friends," says

Christ, "if ye do whatsoever I command you … If ye were of the world, the world would love his own: but because ye are not of the world, but I have chosen you out of the world, therefore the world hateth you." (Ellen G. White, *Our High Calling*, 149)

FEELING PRESSURED TO BE IN A RELATIONSHIP?

For the Lord will help me; therefore I
shall not be confounded: therefore have
I set my face like a flint, and I know that
I shall not be ashamed (Isaiah 50:7).

This is a subject of utmost importance for the single and youth. The single person is already grappling with his or her own issues. Some have a deep sense of what they want, and the qualities they are looking for in a prospective partner. Some don't feel they are ready for a relationship, as they are focused on completing their studies or equipping themselves for a specific line of work or just improving themselves for other plausible reasons. It is extremely confusing, disheartening, and uncomfortable for the single person to feel pressured into a relationship at this juncture of his or her life.

There are family members, coworkers, friends, and church sisters and brothers who, even though well-intentioned, are inflicting severe emotional distress on the single person when they badger the person with questions and statements that suggest that not being in a relationship is a substandard existence. Granted, parents and guardians are encouraged to be involved in the social life of those under their charge. It is also normal for friends to share their views on relationships as they seek to encourage each other on what path to tread on the relationship journey, but constantly harassing and annoying others with sarcastic verbiage and gestures that tend to pressure them into starting relationships when they feel that the timing is not right is wholly unacceptable.

Parents, sensitivity toward your children regarding relationship issues requires that you speak with them intelligently and responsibly. Your tone of voice, choice of words, and the timing of conversations should reflect your understanding of the sensitivity of the subject. Heed the words of wisdom: "Don't exasperate your children" (Colossians 3:21). Exercise care in ensuring that your encouragement is not misconstrued as discouragement, because they feel that you are urging them into a relationship that they are not ready to undertake. Create an open atmosphere where they can freely express their viewpoints in substantiating their position of readiness and preparedness.

Friends and well-wishers, be careful of the joking, bantering approach when confronting the single person on account of his or her social status. Some single persons, in an effort to silence the seething sarcasm and relentless badgering constantly leveled at them, have resorted to surrendering their graceful and chaste lifestyle to one of rebellion and promiscuity. They feel that they have something to prove, and that they are not as weird and "abnormal" as others would want to define them.

As a good soldier of the cross and a caring member of the kingdom of love and grace, be "wise as serpents, and harmless as doves" (Matthew 10:16). Be careful lest you cause one of His children to stumble. Follow the example of Him who represents the standard of brotherhood and camaraderie, and of whom it is said that "a bruised reed shall he not break, and a smoking flax shall he not quench" (Matthew 12:20).

The single person is well advised to remain true to his or her godly enlightened conscience. Set your face as a flint and be true to the conviction that aligns with the Living Word of God. You should seek first to be the right person, and you will be able to discern when the right or the wrong person comes along. Until that day, let the editors publish, let fault-finders quarrel, and let the "lion's roar," but see to it that nothing swerves you from the path that God has chartered for your feet. Let your gaze be as steady as a star, and, as a true sentinel, be as loyal to your God-given duty as the needle to the pole.

MARRIAGE IS ONLY AS GOOD AS YOUR SINGLENESS.

"Have ye not read?" (Matthew 19:4).

Some men tried to ensnare Jesus by asking him a question about divorce. They hoped that, depending on His answer to the question, they would expose Him to the contempt and hatred of the people. They attempted to engage Jesus in a discussion about marriage and divorce, from Moses's perspective. "Didn't Moses recommend a bill of divorcement?" they reasoned. Jesus thought. Instead of focusing on divorce, the end product of a bad marriage, why not consider the rudiments of the preparation of a good marriage? Jesus knew that if they mastered the art of preparation for marriage, there would be no need to preoccupy themselves with thoughts of divorce. Hence, Jesus redirected the discussion to a subject of which they, professing to be prominent teachers of religious creed, should be well aware. They were directed to consider the original Creator of marriage (not Moses), and the principles that undergirded and defined the first marriage. Jesus referred to Genesis 1:27. "God created man in his own image, male and female created he them." God created male and female, not males and females. God made one woman for one man. In this original constitution, no provision was made for divorce or polygamy. Considering that there was only one woman created for one man, Adam could not marry more wives than one, nor could he put her away for any cause. "Have you Pharisees, and all others, not read?"

Jesus was making a point. Spend your time focusing not on the end product of a bad marriage but on the ingredients for a good marriage. For when you have a vital, stable, and triumphant marriage, there is no need for divorce. In other words, the best remedy for divorce is a happy marriage.

What are the ingredients of a good marriage?

For divorce to be possible, there must first be a marriage, and for there to be a marriage, there must first be singles. So the preparation for marriage is singleness. God made Adam and Eve single before they were married, so the quality of their marriage was dependent on whom they were as singles. It is logical to conclude, therefore, that a marriage is only as good as the singleness of those who became married.

There is a lot of instruction here for young lovers. What a man receives in a marriage partner is simply who she was as a single person, and vice versa. There are no magic spells that are wielded when the marital vows are administered. He/she does not change because the person entered a church, no more than visiting the garage turns you into a motorcar. The person he or she was before the wedding, is the same person he or she will be after the wedding. Marriage is like a violin; when the music stops, the strings are still attached. After the wedding bells are hushed and the lights are dimmed, you will still be married to the same person you knew before the marriage.

Oh what solemn thought to ponder. What matter of eternal significance upon which to muse? I hereby pose a question to every single person who cherishes the ambitious hope of getting married someday. Employing the words of Myles Munroe, "If you knew you, the way you know you, would you marry you?" If you would not marry somebody like yourself, then it is time to get to work.

Follow me on this journey, my young friends. While courting with the hope of getting married, do you close your eyes and stop your ears to the signs and signals, and the glaring expression of marital unfitness as demonstrated in your partner? Awake from your slumber, you docile lamb being led to the slaughter. Yes, she looks good, and you are mesmerized by her external attractiveness. You are swept away by her dainty gait as she passes by with pep in her step. The glitter in her eyes has arrested and erupted your deepest emotion, and you declare that she is the one designed by destiny to meet your needs. You vow to have her at any cost, even though the voice of wisdom is speaking with deafening eloquence to the contrary. She opens her mouth when her emotions are bruised and the ridicule, the vulgarity, and the obscenity that drip from her lips send shivers up your spine.

She disagrees with you on some matter, and you can't get a word in as she single-handedly leads the conversation to a deadlock. Her caustic, domineering spirit sends you scurrying for cover. She maligns and wounds, she discredits and disparages everyone that shares a viewpoint contrary to hers, and she continuously teems with bitterness and anger.

You refuse to heed the voice of caution bellowing in your ears that she is wholly unfit as a candidate for marriage, and you move headlong to your destruction, oblivious of the fact that "her house is the way to hell" (Proverbs 7:27). What she needed at that point is not a change of status but a change of heart. Recently, my attention was directed to a statement that read, "A pretty man and a pretty woman make a good wedding, but a righteous man and a virtuous woman make a good marriage."

What about the young lady who fixes her gaze on a member of the opposite sex and determines, whether through desperation or infatuation, to secure the object of her desire at any cost? They commence their romantic adventure, and each is captivated by the sentimental overtures of the other. The young man has had a lifelong habit of being easily angered, and snaps at her for minor incidents of misunderstanding. If she is a minute late for an appointment, he erupts in passionate anger; if she dresses in a manner that is not pleasing to him, he swears and curses. His tone of voice, his choice of words, and his colloquial expressions are symbols of vulgarity, and he rationalizes his impolite demeanor with the explanation that he was born that way, and that's just who he is. She accidentally stepped on his newly acquired pair of expensive shoes or spills her drink on his beautiful shirt, and he responds by raising his hand in a gesture of violence toward her. She is so benumbed by the degree of her desperation that she conveniently ignores the warning signs, convincing herself that he will change once they are married. Oh, simple child of innocence, be you assured of this; if he does not change to get you, don't expect that he'll automatically change to keep you.

You can gauge the quality of the future marriage by the manner in which he resolves conflicts before the marriage. You can predict the imminence of divorce after the wedding by her approach to conflict resolution before the marriage. If as a single person she yells and screams when her wishes are slighted or her demands are not met, then expect to have a contentious wife. Did you know that God is keenly aware of the ordeal that a man endures when he is compelled to live with the wrong woman? Heed His counsel and be not indifferent to His admonition.

> "A continual dropping on a rainy day
> and a contentious woman are alike"
> (Proverbs 27:15).

"It is better to dwell in the corner of the housetop, than with a brawling woman in a wide house" (Proverbs 21:9).

"It is better to dwell in the wilderness, than with a contentious and an angry woman" (Proverbs 21:19).

Men, allow your sail to be propelled by the trade wind of God's word. Allow your vessel to follow the chartered path of the compass of divine council. Marriage is designed to be a lifelong venture, a course from which you should never seek to be graduated. Additionally, marriage was designed to be a harbor in the storm of life, and not a storm in the harbor of life.

Ladies, when you marry, your life, to a large degree, settles for joy or unhappiness. Your wrong choice of a future partner could set you on a path of unimaginable pain and misery in this life and the loss of your eternal heritage in the life to come.

When marriage is being contemplated, there must be no rush, no jostle, no haste or blind navigating. Instead, prayerful deliberation and wise judgment should be carefully engaged.

IN SEARCH OF A FUTURE HUSBAND?

"And from the rib, which the LORD
God had taken from man, made he a
woman, and brought her unto the man"
(Genesis 2:22).

The high rate of divorce in our society today is ample evidence that marriage involves more than just the union of two people that are emotionally attracted to each other. On one of her television shows, *Divorce Court*, Judge Lyn aptly responded in a case brought before her that marriage is "adult stuff." There is in marriage the expression of romance and the exchange of sentimental cordiality. Deeds of kindness and thoughtfulness are freely offered, and words of commendation and appreciation are verbally expressed. But these are just the superstructure. There is need for a solid foundation, without which failure is decidedly assured.

Man, left to himself, is incapable of mastering this art called marriage. We are selfish by nature, and the unregenerate heart enters marriage thinking only of what he can get. "What does this have to offer me?" is the question asked. But a marriage built on selfishness is bound to fail. A successful marriage requires the union of two people whose hearts have been flushed, cleansed, and purified of selfishness, and the vacuum filled with the panacea of the Holy Spirit, the only remedy capable of refreshing and restoring the qualities needed for a triumphant marriage. God spoke poignantly on this subject: "But the fruit of the Spirit is love, joy, peace, long-suffering, gentleness, goodness, faith" (Galatians 5:22).

For marriage to be successful there is need for love, the "agape," unconditional, and sacrificial love. Search the world over, examine every philanthropic source, or converse with every modern philosopher, and you will discover no other source from which this love can be derived except the Holy Spirit of the Living God. Man cannot manufacture it, regardless of his class or caste, his moral or academic endowment, or his social or economic status, and any attempt to consummate a marriage without this love will leave you bewildered and deluded.

Where then do you begin? What is your first and principal duty? The message of the scriptural text is clarion clear. God made a woman and brought her unto the man. He led, conducted, and presented her to Adam. The word implies a solemn bestowment in the bonds of the marriage covenant. For God to bring Eve to Adam, then Eve must first be in God's hand. Eve did not know where Adam was, but God knew where Adam was. Similarly, you do not know where Mr. Right is. But if you place yourself in God's hand, God, who knows where Mr. Right is, will take you to Mr. Right. So your first duty is not to go "man hunting," but "God hunting," and if your hand is in God's hand, He who knows where Mr. Right is will take you to Mr. Right.

I recently listened to the exciting story of a young woman, featured on Dr. James Dobson's *Family Talk* radio program. She is renowned singer and author Rebecca St. James. The program was conducted under the caption: "Singleness, Waiting for God's best." Rebecca spoke of her experience of being single for a relatively long time, before she met her "knight in shining armor." She spoke of the struggle of single living and the rewards of doing it right. Rebecca indicated how much she thought longingly of the day when she would be married, but was willing, against all odds, to wait patiently on God's timing. She shared a few tips: (1) trust God, love Him, and continue to be faithful to him; (2) Get out of your comfort zone, fix yourself up, and be proactive in Christian community. In other words, get busy with God's work, and interacting with God's people.

At the time of the interview, she expressed that she was happily married, which was a testimony of God's faithfulness to those who wait patiently for Him. The lesson here is that the principle of entrusting oneself to God's leadership is still the best method in navigating the uncharted path of the premarriage adventure (*Family Talk*, with Dr. James Dobson, "Singleness: Waiting for God's Best, Part 1").

IN SEARCH OF A FUTURE WIFE?

> And the LORD God took the man, and
> put him into the garden of Eden to dress
> it and to keep it. And the LORD God
> commanded the man, saying, "of every
> tree of the garden thou mayest freely
> eat: But of the tree of the knowledge of
> good and evil, thou shalt not eat of it: for
> in the day that thou eatest thereof thou
> shalt surely die" (Genesis 2:15–17).

It is not recorded anywhere in scripture where God ever communicated His instructions for the human race directly to Eve, the first woman, the mother of the race. God spoke to Adam. God sought to adequately equip Adam so he would be prepared to lead a fulfilled life, imparting divine counsel to his family. God spoke to Adam while he was single, and as far as Adam was concerned, he never felt as though he needed anyone. He felt a sense of completeness before God.

Before God blessed man with a woman, He gave him two things, namely: work and His word (Genesis 2:15–18). God gave him work, intending to endow him with a sense of responsibility and industry, for he would need these qualities to aid him in caring for a family. God bequeathed to man His Word, teaching him that he must first be an example of uprightness and righteousness, so that by precept and example he could communicate this Word to his wife and children. It is interesting to note that in Genesis 3:2–3 Eve communicated to the serpent the same message that was given to Adam prior to her appearance on the scene. The text implies that Eve's knowledge of God's command as communicated by her to the serpent in Genesis 3:2–3 was conveyed to her by her husband.

It is God's will that the man possesses God's Word, so that he will be able to subsequently communicate it to his family. It is easy to understand why the man is considered the priest, or the spiritual head of the home. Joshua, a faithful husband and father, echoed a compelling message down through the corridors of time when he announced, "Choose you this day whom ye will serve … but as for me and my house, we will serve the LORD" (Joshua 24:15).

Therefore, you are a single man. Where do you place your first step? Your first and principal duty is to align yourself with God, so, as with Adam, He can communicate to you His word, even before He gives you a wife. I entreat you earnestly, brother; seek God before you seek a wife. God will make Himself responsible for leading, conducting, and presenting you with a woman of virtue. Remember His promise: "Houses and riches are the inheritance from fathers: and a prudent wife is from the Lord" (Proverbs 19:14).

If you fail to follow the divine sequence.

If by rash impulse or stubborn determination, you shake your puny fist in the face of God in defiance and rebellion, as though you are capable to be the arbiter of your own destiny, then don't be surprised if you are later condemned to take up your cross and bear it, in the wrong choice of a life partner. And ladies need to be equally warned. A man who does not first and foremost align himself with God's word, and is living in obedience to the counsel of Holy Writ, is not qualified to take your hand in marriage. My brothers, old and young alike, heed the counsel of divine wisdom, and goodness and mercy shall follow thee all the days of thy life.

UNEQUALLY YOKED?

Are you a believer in a relationship with
an unbeliever?

So you are a believer in a relationship with an unbeliever, and it is your earnest contemplation to eventually seal the union in the holy estate of matrimony? The Lord your God, who loves you with an everlasting love, would like to have audience with you. There is a marriage that is unto the Lord, and a union between a believer and an unbeliever is certainly not that marriage. The Lord has spoken unequivocally on the subject. The earnestness of His plea and the compelling force of His admonition are commensurate with his depth of love for you and His desire for your happiness and well-being. He admonishes, "What harmony is there between Christ and Belial? Or what does a believer have in common with an unbeliever? (2

Corinthians 6:15, NIV). Can two walk together, except they be agreed? (Amos 3:3). Whom will you follow: The natural inclination of your own heart already ablaze with sheer sentimentalism and blind passion, or will you follow the counsel of divine wisdom that foresees the end from the beginning?

Are you being infatuated by her winsome exterior? Are you hypnotized by his cordial gestures and flattering words, causing you to silence the prompting of God's spirit with the thought, "He pleases me well"? Oh innocent one, a trap is laid for your feet. A snare is made for your soul that you cannot discern. There may be some who have managed to escape the perils of this risky adventure, but they are in the miniscule minority. Do not massage your soul with the thought that you'll be able to convert him to the Lord once the marriage knot is tied. It may be far more difficult than you imagine. The fact is if he will not change to get you, then he won't change to keep you. If you were purchasing a house, you would put forth earnest effort to ensure its safety for human habitation. You would even insist that the inspector ascertain that its foundation does not rest on a sinkhole. Will you be less thorough in ensuring that the union to which you will commit the rest of your life is on a solid foundation?

Research the life of King Solomon. He received explicit prohibition against forming an emotional alliance with the heathen nation. He disobeyed God and won the heart of pharaoh's daughter, with whom he subsequently exchanged marital vows. As a result of that union, his usefulness as a servant of God was compromised, and his life became a symbol of heartache and misery. I was so moved by this chapter in the life of Solomon that I shared this story with my family in worship this morning. I led my sons in a drill asking them to repeat this line ten times: "You cannot disobey God and win, but, on the contrary, if you obey God, you will win."

My friends, resist the urge to follow the path of blind impulse and stubborn determination. Your happiness is at stake, and your eternal destiny lies in the balance. Speak with those who have tread this path, and almost always they will lament that rivers of tears, mountains of problems, and acres of heartaches have been their lot. Don't force your way through a door that has been bolted by the expressed prohibition of God. Don't toy with the devil and call it holy festivity.

God declared to Amaziah through the prophet that whatsoever you give up for the Lord's sake, "The Lord is able to give thee much more than this" (2 Chronicles

25:9). Heed the counsel of divine wisdom. Reject the diabolical promptings of the evil one. Fall at the feet of your loving Jesus. He will hear you when you call; He will lift you when you fall. He has an eye for your success and a heart for your happiness. He's interested in your well-being. His insurance is, "For I know the plans I have for you, plans to prosper you and not to harm you, plans to give you hope and a future (Jeremiah 29:11, NIV).

If he/she does not like the presence of God and you enjoy his/her presence, then something is wrong with your profession of faith.

PICK THE RIGHT PERSON, NOT JUST THE CONVENIENT PERSON.

Don't foster the development of a relationship that you know is going nowhere. Many form relationships due to proximity or convenience. Some argue that establishing a relationship with a neighbor or coworker has worked well for them, as they are able to keenly scrutinize the behavior and lifestyle of the person. Some of these relationships have been translated into great success stories. The fact is if you had a standard, and this suitor or secret admirer had "measured up," then there is the green light to proceed.

But others have formed relationships due to convenience. This is not the person that they or their parents or grandparents would have recommended under other circumstances, but they just leached on to each other because Mr. or Mrs. Right has not yet arrived, and they claim they must "occupy till he comes." You should pose a few questions to yourself if you are involved in a relationship of this sort.

1. Am I wasting my time?

You spend much precious time in each other's company. In the deep recesses of your soul, you know it to be a settled fact that this relationship is going nowhere, but you are just hanging on to him/her as a temporary "fill-in." Could it be that you are wasting valuable hours that you could invest in meaningful employment or some endeavor calculated to improve or enhance yourself?

2. Am I encouraging the cementing of emotions and the strengthening of a bond that we both will find difficult to disentangle later?

Paraphrasing the words of a song I heard many years ago, memories don't live like people do; they always stay with you. Furthermore, parents, relatives, friends, and well-wishers have been brought into the mix, and they have begun their round of expressing their sentiments and wishes for the relationship. They have expectations, and you subsequently find it difficult to disappoint them. How easily you could wake up to the rude awakening that you are finally wedded to a person that you in a million years would not have selected to own your affection "until death do us part." Now you are trapped, and you find it difficult to escape.

3. Have I received favors from him/her that I feel obligated to return?

We have not yet ascended to the realms of angels, and so it is seldom that you find a person who will render favors without expecting something in return. Not that it is impossible, but it is rare. He/she has sacrificed so much of his time, talent, and resources, and he feels unjustly treated if you should disappear from his grasp or leave him "in the cold." Oh what a tangled web you have woven. You have lingered too long under the forbidden tree, and now you feel pressured into eating forbidden fruit. Be wise, my soul, and apply thine heart unto wisdom.

4. What about engaging in activities that could become problematic for a healthy relationship later?

Many lose their virginity and sacrifice their dignity to a relationship that they knew was going nowhere. Is it worth it? The answer is an emphatic no. Some have become pregnant, contracted communicable diseases, exposed themselves to shame and ridicule, and have even interrupted their educational pursuits and development permanently. "Teach us to number our days," the divine record admonishes, "that we may apply our hearts unto wisdom" (Psalm 90:12).

FLEE FORNICATION.

"Flee fornication" (1 Corinthians 6:18).

This is a subject of utmost importance. The magnitude of its implication and the profundity of its meaning are staggering. It is mind-boggling that a violation of the divine order, a deviation from the rule of chastity, and an act that represents a deathly blow to the body and soul, should be practiced with such levity and impunity. This is not a sin such as gluttony, drunkenness, or self-murder, which are "without," or comparatively external to the body.

Mark 7:21–23 declares that "from within, out of the heart of men, proceed evil thoughts, adulteries, fornications. All these evil thoughts come from within and defile the man."

Proverbs 6:32 asserts that whosoever "committeh adultery with a woman lacketh understanding: he that doeth it destroyeth his own soul."

Jemieson-Fausett-Brown Bible Commentary elucidates the concept as found in 1 Corinthians 6:18: "Fornication alienates that body which is the Lord's and makes it one with a harlot's body, and so sins against his own body that is against Verity and the nature of his body, not a mirror effect on the body from without but a contradiction of the truth of the body from within itself."

The force of scripture on this subject defies our ability to fathom or fully comprehend it, but suffice it to say it is a weighty matter in God's reckoning. The biblical record informs us that the children of Israel, a vast number of them, committed fornication, and fell in one day three and twenty thousand (RH April 18, 1893, par. 11).

In his book *Love, Sex and Relationship*, Chip Ingram has an important word of encouragement for those that are virgins when he proclaimed that being a virgin isn't weird, but instead it's profoundly wise. He posed a challenge to his reading audience, by asking, "If I could tell you how to avoid sexually transmitted diseases;

how to give your marriage a 50 percent better chance of surviving; and how to live a guiltless, healthy and satisfying life, would you be interested?" He returned with an answer that is inconsistent with the hype of Hollywood: "It begins with sexual purity—virginity."

How does this sin impact my fitness for the eternal inheritance?

All unrighteousness is sin. All reigning sin committed with design and not repented of shuts a person out of the kingdom of heaven. "Be not deceived," cautions the biblical record. Let's not flatter ourselves that we may live in sin yet die in Christ and receive a welcome through the gates into the city of God in the hereafter.

"But if we confess and forsake our sin, He is faithful and just to forgive our sins and to cleanse us of all unrighteousness" (1 John 1:9).

The blood of Christ and the washing of regeneration can take away all guilt (Titus 3:5).

"There hath no temptation taken you but such as is common to man; but God who is faithful, who will not suffer you to be tempted above that ye are able; but will with the temptation also make a way to escape, that ye may be able to bear it" (1 Corinthians 10:13).

Strict adherence to moral principle is our only safeguard and shield. We must constantly be receiving strength from above in unbroken communion with the Holy Spirit if we are to restrain our passion and emerge as victors in this moral, social, and emotional combat with the enemy of souls. As fellow members of the household of faith and heirs of a spiritual heritage, we must be constantly encouraging one another. We are reminded in scripture to consider one another to provoke unto love and to good works. See Hebrews 10:24.

The fact is, friends, we are living amid the perils of the last day. Iniquity abounds everywhere we roam. Immorality seems to be the order of the day to the extent that giving public expression of our loving relationship with Jesus may isolate us or expose us to the unkind treatment of others. We must recognize that we are engaged in hand-to-hand warfare with a diabolical foe. Many who were once considered the spiritually prominent among us are losing their hold and becoming weak and frail, even rationalizing their mediocre stance on religious matters.

Many are drowning spiritually as the waves of sin continue to rise. Peer pressure, the prevailing music of the popular media, the fun and frolic of secular society, the insinuation of ungodly friends and acquaintances, and the temptation of unscrupulous business engagements are doing a perfect work. The temptations we have to contend with in this modern society are more subtle, imperceptible, and vicious than many realize or discern. If we relax our vigilance, then even the elect are at risk of being overcome and eternally lost.

Oh for a double portion of the Spirit of the Living God to remove the scales from our eyes so we may see clearly, to sharpen our perception of right and wrong, to fortify our minds with supernatural power, and to strengthen our resolve in obedience to God.

"Intensify our hunger, dear Lord so we may seek divine nourishment for our emaciated soul, and help us to search for you as for hid treasure."

DOES HE OR SHE FORCE YOU TO ENGAGE IN SEXUAL ACTIVITY PRIOR TO MARRIAGE?

A young man, and to a lesser extent the young lady, toys with the idea that "everybody is doing it," so it is not only understood but acceptable if I give expression to my body's surging hormones and compelling sexual desire. Hence he/she finds no issue in coercing another person into premarital sexual activity.

Whenever this happens, the young person at that point in time has had the intellectual side of his brain, the section that controls reason (the neocortex) hijacked by the emotional side of the brain (the amygdala). He does not care about what others think of him—that he is selfish, caring only about the gratification of his own feelings without regard for the other's health, future, or well-being.

This section of his brain that controls reason does not wrestle with reality, considering that a sexually transmitted disease could be communicated, or one person could get pregnant and thus drastically alter his/her personal development and aspiration. One or both persons may drop out of school, as they are forced to care for a child for the next eighteen years, at least. One or both persons could also risk losing a job or compromising their reputation with their church or other organization, or society in general. There is also the possibility of homelessness, as some may be unkindly treated by parents and guardians, and are ordered to leave home with no destination in sight.

Whenever a person forces another into premarital sexual activity, the person is really saying, "I have such scant regard for your welfare that it does not matter what happens to you as a consequence of this act," or the person might be saying in effect, "I care about gratifying my feelings to the extent that I don't care about your future." This is not only a misnomer but an infinitely selfish act that is instigated by the enemy of our soul, the arch-deceiver and destroyer of the human heart.

I implore all my young friends. Whenever you stand at the crossroad of making a decision that will affect your life, health, and destiny, make yourself evaluate before you participate. Count the cost. Consider the pros and cons. Think about the people that you will disappoint. Think about the career, the reputation, and the family that you risk losing. Most importantly, think about the relationship with God (the only one that gives life true meaning and stability), that you will rupture. Jesus was separated from his parents in the temple in a few moments, yet it took him three days to be reunited with them. The momentary act that shatters your relationship with God today could cost you a protracted period of painful ordeal before you are reunited in a vibrant and vital relationship with Him.

This act of resisting temptation, fleeing fornication, and turning your back on sin found Joseph leaving his coat in the hands of a seductive Potiphar's wife. Reason with your own soul today. Contemplate eternal realities, and chime in with the songwriter (particularly on the refrain):

> 1. One thing I of the Lord desire,
> For all my path hath miry been,
> Be it by water or by fire,
> O make me clean, O make me clean.

[Refrain]
Wash me, Thou, without, within,
Or purge with fire, if that must be,
Anyhow, if only sin
Die out in me, die out, die out in me.

2. If clearer vision Thou impart,
Grateful and glad my soul shall be;
But yet to have a purer heart
Is more to me, is more to me.
[Refrain]

3. Yea, only as this heart is clean
May larger vision yet be mine,
For mirrored in its depths are seen
The things divine, the things divine.
[Refrain]

4. I watch to shun the miry way,
And stanch the springs of guilty thought,
But, watch and struggle as I may,
Pure I am not, pure I am not.
[Refrain]

—Walter Charmer Smith

RESTRAIN (CURB) THE URGE

Sex is like fire in a fireplace. When it's contained and controlled, it is a benefit and a blessing. But when it is allowed to burn and exhibit itself without restraint, it can set the entire house ablaze and cause incalculable damage.

Sex is not cheap. Sex is not for the reckless and careless. There is a high price tag attached to sex.

Only those who engage in sex with a realization of God's design will understand its joy and purpose in human relationship. God has a multifaceted purpose for creating sex. He has given sex to us as a means of glorifying Him as we fulfill its design for procreation, intimacy, comfort, and physical pleasure. Sex is a fulfillment of God's created design in marriage between a husband and wife.

The Architect, the Manufacturer, the Designer of sex is the only one suited to give unequivocal instruction (like the manufacturer of a car) regarding the "how" and "why" of sex. It was God who made the first man and woman and brought them together into the holy estate of matrimony. They were both naked and not ashamed. This everlasting creator, full of grace and truth, the embodiment of wisdom and understanding, bequeathed to us guidelines regarding the proper use of sex.

God intended that sex be engaged in only by those who, in a monogamous marital relationship, have committed themselves to each other's joy, delight, and fulfillment. His admonition on the subject is unmistakable: "Nevertheless, to avoid fornication, let every man have his own wife, and let every woman have her own husband. Let the husband render unto the wife her due [benevolence]; and likewise also, the wife unto the husband" (1 Corinthians 7:2–3). "Marriage is honorable in all, and the bed undefiled" (Hebrews 13:4). "Therefore shall a man leave his father and his mother, and shall cleave unto his wife: and they shall be one flesh" (Genesis 2:24).

My friends, with words as gentle as the dew drops and as bold as the roar of a lion, I echo the sentiment of divine love and compassion. Hear the preacher. Refuse to heed the counsel of Holy Writ from the architect himself regarding sex, and our hearts will resonate the heartache, our bodies will bear the infirmities, and our souls will mourn the guilt and shame as the wages of our disobedience are paid out in copious and immeasurable dividends.

Curb the urge, restrain the impulse, control the emotion and hold in check the raging hormones. Do it for yourself, your children, and your children's children. Save a generation from the pangs of incurable communicable diseases, the ills of birth defects, the wailing cry of unplanned families, and a society riddled with heinous crime and violence from fatherless, motherless, and improperly trained children. Curb the urge, and save yourself a lifetime of heartache, misery and painful regret. Curb the urge as you patiently await the arrival of the prince or princess in shining armor or glistening gems. Restrain the impulse even if he or she were never to arrive.

Count the cost, ponder your moves, and time will confirm that it's better to be clean and blessed than to be messed up and wretched. Let's be real. It is still better to be a happy single than a miserable double.

Sex is not cheap.

Sex carries a price.

Sex is for responsible people.

We have a duty to guard our bodies.

HOW DO I CURB THE URGE?

"Whatsoever things are pure … lovely …
and of good report … think on these
things" (Philippians 4:8).

Every desire for love or sexual expression is triggered and initiated in the brain. The brain is the control center for every bodily system and function. The thoughts are a product of mental activity from which the actions are generated. It's logical to conclude that if we control our thoughts, we can control our actions. In this sex-crazed world, where almost everything is advertised or promoted using sex labels, symbols, or innuendos, a person is constantly bombarded with thoughts about sex.

Many people are in jail today because they give free rein to their passion, or failed to control their thoughts.

They are called "offenders" because the uncontrolled behavior resulting from uncontrolled thoughts and impulses translated into offensive acts toward others. "Where shall a young man cleanse his ways?" is the question asked. "By giving heed to the word of God" (Psalm 119:9), comes the answer fraught with divine authority. When thoughts about sex arise in the mind, you apply the principle of displacement or the expulsive power of a new affection. This is done by allowing mental concepts to dominate the thought process. A married man or woman, for example, allows the principle of fidelity to his spouse to control the reins of his mind when bombarded with thoughts of sex. A single person who is busy with wholesome employment or activity has enough to occupy his/her mind, so his/her thoughts about sex are kept in subjection. As a general principle, the person who is in the habit of fortifying the mind with earnest study of the word of God is not only possessed with lofty and enduring principles to positively impact his thoughts but is also empowered by the supernatural influence of the Author of the word himself, the Holy Spirit.

A single person who is serious about curbing the urge cannot frequent places that inspire a desire for sexual stimulation. He will discover that the movie houses, the pleasure parties, the disco clubs, and the dance hall extravaganza do not assist him but instead hijack the rational sensors of the brain, benumb the senses, and imperceptibly drown him in behavior calculated to destroy his manhood or her feminine dignity.

Statistics have consistently confirmed that the incidence of rape on college campuses is far more than is reported, and they usually occur when young people are invited to these places of amusement, duped with drugs, and led away as sheep to the slaughter. The majority of people who are currently alcoholics and smokers started the habit while they were still teenagers. They were influenced by peers, while visiting pleasure spots, movie theaters, and amusement sites where the angels of God could not accompany them.

Being serious about "curbing the urge" means you will not read books or listen to music that rivets the mind with unwholesome thoughts about sex. The senses are the avenues to the mind. Be extremely careful, yea intentional, about what you allow your senses to feed upon, for so will your thoughts and subsequently your actions be controlled. Don't test yourself. You may not be as strong as you think you are.

"Thy word have I hid in my heart that I might not sin against thee" (Psalm 119:11).

"Flee fornication" (1 Thessalonians 4:3).

ABSTAIN FROM SEX AND ALL THAT LEADS TO SEX.

"Lead us not into temptation, but deliver us from evil" (Matthew 6:13).

This should be the prayer of every single person who is intentional about maintaining sexual purity. Genuinely making this request of God implies that you desire to live, act, and behave according to the sentiments of your prayer. In other words, you should be cooperating with God as you seek the fulfillment of your earnest entreaty. It is a misnomer to be reading love novels while trying to be abstinent. Watching movies with explicit love scenes and reading books and periodicals that depict illicit sexual activities are no help to single believers. Listening to music with lewd and sexually charged lyrics is not a friend of grace to help you on to God.

God must have been referring to these obstacles in our pilgrimage when he declared that if "your right eye offend you then pluck it out" (Matthew 5:29). If there is a plank in your eye or a thorn in your flesh, or if there is noise that troubleth your Christian serenity or gall that sours the taste buds, then what is your duty? Books on your shelves, compact discs in your stereo, and a movie on your screen, but your soul is tending toward perdition. It's time for action. Light a fire if you must, but cast the whole lot of them into the bottomless pit and remember them no more. You could be saving your soul from destruction and your family from the fires of hell.

To the single, unmarried person:

Abstain from sex and all that leads to sex.

FINDING HEALING AFTER SEXUAL IMMORALITY

The David and Bathsheba Saga

David is not exempt from the compelling passion and fiery urge that adorn the loins of every normal man on the planet.

Some may refrain from talking about it; others will not admit its existence, and still others are too shy to discuss it.

There are married couples who fail to initiate a discussion about sex even within the privacy of their own bedroom, though ignoring a discussion of the subject is severely injuring the emotional stability of their relationship.

How could a king, a prince of God, and an esteemed preacher of righteousness and proclaimer of the Word fall a victim of sex, an act that seems so insignificant that members in the Christian church don't care to talk about it. So minuscule is this pebble of a temptation (or so we think) that some parents overlook it when interacting with their children, or shove it aside as almost nonexistent. Yet this mighty man of valor and the civic leader of a great nation found it too boisterous and ferocious to control.

Like a tornado, the relentless thought of sex rumbles across the millions of cells in his brain, attacking the neurotransmitters and setting ablaze the flammable dopamine that consumes like a burning bush. All it took was one look at the fatal beauty of Bathsheba, and the prefrontal cortex in the frontal lobe of the brain was hijacked, crippling his sense of good decision and proper judgment.

Like the paralyzing glare of a laser beam, the amygdala in the rear of his brain that is connected with the emotion gained mastery and struck his soul, and he immediately forgot that he was standing on a royal platform as the enforcer and the proclaimer of moral and civic laws. David had one thing on his mind, not how to win another war or perform a sacrificial service on the holy altar, but to chase the "dopamine high" that is triggered in his brain and to release the tension of his normal physiology.

He ventured like a blind man driving a racing car. He couldn't see clearly, having been blinded by lust and infatuation. "All I want is to have her, to feel her caress, to bask in her warmth, and to revel in her romance." His rational mind attempted to nudge him: "You are risking all, your position as ruler of Israel, your reputation as an eminent teacher of righteousness, and your dignity as head of a great family."

I heard his lips speaking in protest as though instructed by his confused emotional self. "I don't care; I'm like a drunken man. I'll discuss that later—at a more convenient season. I've got to go; pleasure is summoning me, and thrill, joy, and ecstasy are all waiting to greet me. Wow, it's a great feeling. Heaven has visited earth. I love her. I love her. I want her and that's it. It doesn't matter anymore." The chapter is closed, and the die is cast. Thank you. Thank you.

The ultimate happened. David crossed the line. The record says David slept with Bathsheba.

David didn't set out to commit an insidious sin. People seldom do. At first inquiry, he didn't know this woman's identity or her marital status. Had she been unmarried, he would have been quite proper in pursuing her as a wife, and his inquiry would not have been improper. By the time he learned that she was married, David had already let lust get its nasty little hooks into his heart, and his lustful desire outweighed his good sense and integrity. Unbridled lust can do that to a person—yes, even you, if you allow it to smolder long enough. By this point, it's apparent that David's intentions have shifted from an interest in taking Bathsheba as a wife, to just plain taking Bathsheba. David had no plans on a long-term affair—just a one-night sexual romp with a good-looking woman.1

> "And the woman conceived, and sent and told David, and said, I am with child" (2 Samuel 11:5).

David paid a high price for casual or uncontrolled sex.

In his attempt to cover up the sin, he laid a carefully devised plan that would lead to the death of Uriah, Bathsheba's husband. What a tangled web we weave when first we decide to deceive. Not only was he now guilty of adultery, but his hands were stained with blood—he was also guilty of murder.

And he wrote in the letter, saying, "Set ye Uriah in the forefront of the hottest battle, and retire ye from him, that he may be smitten, and die." 16 And it came to pass, when Joab observed the city, that he assigned Uriah unto a place where he knew that valiant men were. 17 "And the men of the city went out, and fought with Joab: and there fell some of the people of the servants of David, and Uriah the Hittite died also. And when the wife of Uriah heard that Uriah her husband was dead, she mourned for her husband. And when the mourning was past, David sent and fetched her to his house, and she became his wife, and bare him a son. But the thing that David had done displeased the LORD" (2 Samuel 11:15–17, 26–27).

David, by his sin, tended to lower the standard of godliness in Israel.

David's sin misrepresented the character of God and cast reproach upon His name. It tended to lower the standard of godliness in Israel, to lessen in many minds the abhorrence of sin; while those who did not love and fear God were by it emboldened in transgression.2

"By this deed you have given occasion to the enemies of the LORD to blaspheme" (2 Samuel 12:14a).

David was unable to effectively perform the duties of his office in denouncing sin in others, considering he was just as guilty.

His son died.

"The child also that is born to you shall surely die" (2 Samuel 12:14b).

Disgrace was brought upon his house by his own family.

The judgment proclaimed upon David's household came to pass:

> "Thus saith the LORD, Behold, I will raise up evil against thee out of thine own house, and I will take thy wives before thine eyes, and give them unto thy neighbor, and he shall lie with thy wives in the sight of this sun. For thou didst it secretly: but I will do this thing before all Israel, and before the sun." (2 Samuel 12:11–12).

David's rebellious son Absalom publicly went in to his father's wives and concubines to demonstrate his rebellion to the nation (2 Samuel 16:20–22).

David was driven from the throne.

In humility and sorrow, David passed out of the throne of Jerusalem—driven from his throne, from his palace, from the ark of God, by the insurrection of his cherished son. The people followed in long, sad procession, like a funeral train.3

If Nathan had not confronted and rebuked David, he would have been ruined.

The Bible is replete with the message, from Genesis to Revelation, that God's principal mission is one of restoration and healing.

His repentance was deep and genuine.

"And David said unto Nathan, I have sinned against the LORD" (2 Samuel 12:13).

He did not try to play the "blame game." He took responsibility for his own action—his own sin.

David Restored to Friendship with God

The element in David's heart that made him a man after God's own heart rose up within him. He knew that he could not hide one jot or tittle of his sins from God, for God sees in the dark as clearly as in the noonday. He knew that the only remedy for his sin was to "come clean," and lay his soul bare before the inspecting eye of God. He was also keenly aware of the importance of being honest with himself. Genuine repentance and a determination to reform are the only formula by which we can seek reconciliation with our fellow men and with God.

It does not matter the nature of the sin that you have committed. It is not too large or obnoxious for God to extinguish. It does not matter how deep you have fallen; God's hand can reach to the lowest valley. It does not matter how long you have played the fool; God knew that your effort to find wisdom without Him was futile. Remember this; where sin abounds, God's grace doth much more abound. If you, in humility and soul hunger, cry to God for forgiveness and cleansing and strength to rise again, He will hear and answer, and you shall come forth as pure gold. This is His promise: "Call unto me, and I will answer thee, and shew thee great and mighty things, which thou knowest not" (Jeremiah 33:3).

David's Impassioned Plea to God
for Forgiveness and Cleansing

"Create in Me a Clean Heart, O
God" (2 Samuel 12:1–12).

[To the chief musician, a Psalm of David, when
Nathan the prophet came unto him, after he had gone
in to Bathsheba.]

> Have mercy upon me, O God, according to thy
> loving-kindness: according unto the multitude
> of thy tender mercies blot out my transgressions.

> Wash me thoroughly from mine iniquity, and
> cleanse me from my sin.

> For I acknowledge my transgressions: and my
> sin is ever before me.

> Against thee, thee only, have I sinned, and
> done this evil in thy sight: that thou mightest
> be justified when thou speakest, and be clear
> when thou judgest.

> Behold, I was shapen in iniquity; and in sin did
> my mother conceive me.

Behold, thou desirest truth in the inward parts: and in the hidden part thou shalt make me to know wisdom.

Purge me with hyssop, and I shall be clean: wash me, and I shall be whiter than snow.

Make me to hear joy and gladness; that the bones which thou hast broken may rejoice.

Hide thy face from my sins, and blot out all mine iniquities.

Create in me a clean heart, O God; and renew a right spirit within me.

Cast me not away from thy presence; and take not thy holy spirit from me.

Restore unto me the joy of thy salvation; and uphold me with thy free spirit.

David—A Man after God's Own Heart

David's experience provides a comforting assurance that if we seek God earnestly in the moment of our most trying circumstances, He will hear and answer, and restore us to sweet fellowship with Himself.

David was reckoned a man after God's own heart because, though met with retribution for his sins, he never blamed others for his mishap, nor protested against God or His counsel. Instead he was humble and serene knowing that the only means of remedying his condition was securing once again the favor of God. He desired more than anything else to be in a harmonious relationship with God.

If you roamed recklessly from the sacred portals of your marriage and have been unfaithful to your spouse. If you have defiled your body temple by engaging in casual or uncontrolled sex, I implore you on the authority of God's word and the immutability of David's God that if you surrender in contrition and sorrow for your sins, and plead for God's forgiveness, He will cleanse you as with hyssop, and you shall be clean.

God restored unto David a happy family.

God demonstrated His grace in the sanctification of a relationship that had once brought the condemnation of death. The union with Bathsheba brought forth Solomon, a child regarded by both sacred and secular authority as one of the wisest men ever born. He succeeded his father as king, and his name appears in the direct bloodline of Christ in the New Testament genealogies. The restored, healed, sanctified marriage of David and Bathsheba bears both God's hand and His blessing. It is important to note that the healing and reconstruction of this relationship did not happen immediately. Based on historical accounts and comparative scriptural studies, it is apparent that several years passed between the death of the first son and the birth of Solomon. It is also apparent that, although David had many wives, Bathsheba became his favorite. A marriage built on the healing grace of God always produces very special, intimate, bonded relationships.4

Finding Healing after Infidelity

Your relationship may be tainted with the stain of infidelity. Your heart throbbed with the pain of betrayal, and you feel like calling it quits. You might have been encouraged by family and friends alike to close that chapter in your experience and move on. Just before you draw the line, however, please allow me to encourage your heart and to share with you another perspective.

The incidence of infidelity does not necessarily mean that the marriage has failed. It is still possible to reconstruct a "new marriage with the same person." If you are truly desirous of repairing the breach and mending the brokenness, then find it in your heart to approach the partner that you have wronged, and in contrition and genuine sorrow for your sin, ask for forgiveness. Let him/her know that you are aware that you have caused pain and distress, and from the depth of your soul, you are sorry. Then you must convey the assurance that if given another chance, you pledge, by God's grace, to be faithful to him/her in thought, word, and deed.

To the offended party, I would say, give the matter careful thought, and don't be in a rush to throw away something that God's power is able to restore, especially if reconciliation with your spouse would not prove a threat to your life, health, or safety. Many people make a decision against restoration and reconciliation with their spouses because of the hardness of their hearts. (See Matthew 19:8.) The same God who made marriage can re-create marriage. With hard work and commitment, your marriage can become a success story, even after infidelity.

Our Only Safety

Our only safety in this life is living in harmony with God and His expressed principles. History is replete with examples of those who have challenged the wisdom of God's counsel and the sadness, pain, heartache, and hopelessness that mark their existence. The quest to amass wealth must not be your principal aim. The pursuit of romance and sex beyond the borders of marriage must never be a consuming ambition of your life. Instead seek an understanding of the body mechanism with which God has blessed you, so you may be aware of what is required for its proper maintenance and upkeep as the temple of God. Seek an understanding of what God requires of you as His own property, and align yourself to live in conformity to His will. If you do these things, you shall never fail, but you will enjoy the fullness of life in this world and the world to come.

SINGLE PARENTING

Children are gifts from God.

As a single mom or dad, you are the sole custodian of the children in the home. This is an honorable and a challenging task. It is a task most honorable because you are a steward and a representative of God to your children. God has conferred upon you the honor of training young minds and shaping the destiny of innocent lives. Children, the Master announces, are a heritage from the Lord (Psalm 127:3). They are gifts, not burdens. In your children, God has endowed you with talents to improve for the blessing of humanity, faculties to develop for the betterment of the world, and minds to cultivate for fitness into the everlasting kingdom. Regardless of your religious affiliation or moral status, this special duty must not be treated with scant regard.

They are lent treasures.

If you reckon your children as gifts from above, then your manner of relating to them will reflect this thought, and they in turn will mirror the worth and importance with which they are treated. They are not burdens; they are not afterthoughts, but they are precious jewels to be loved, respected, and cared for. When you awake in the morning, and you behold your children, replicas of your mortal image, is your heart filled with love for them? Is your soul brimming with rapturous joy and delight that in your hand is the power to change the world for good in the proper care and management of these gems of epic potential? Is your heart warmed by their genuine smiles and warm hugs in response to a gentle word of commendation and appreciation from your lips? They skip and jump about with a joyful gait, giving expression to your intervention in their physical and emotional well-being. Aren't you overwhelmed with a sense of appreciation and gratitude to God for considering you worthy enough to endow you with mortal lives to impact for time and eternity?

Hannah's life (see 1 Samuel 1:20, 27–28) prefigures the partnership God intended when He blessed us with offspring. God stands as Creator and Owner, while parents are considered stewards endowed with talents to improve for his kingdom. We will be required to account for the quality of the preparation of our children to meet the challenging issues of life. While Samuel was still a child, his mother, Hannah vowed to God that she would train the child aright as she graciously returns him to his Maker. She carefully taught him to distinguish between good and evil. As a result of this early training, his mind was "garrisoned in the hour of fierce temptation and he was able to choose to maintain his Christian integrity." (CG, 197.2). The operative question to ponder is, "How will I answer to God for the little flock that He has entrusted to my care?"

Be a model of what you want your children to become.

The scripture aptly instructs us that out of the abundance of the heart the mouth speaks. Luke 6:45. Did you know that when the heart is profuse with the heavenly fragrance and saturated with the spiritual graces then you readily appreciate those attributes when manifested in other lives? If the heart is to experience the fullness of the divine attributes, then we must be drinking from the living stream that flows directly from the heart of God.

Parents, it is not really our children that make us angry and upset. They have only touched the right button that reveals the inadequacy of our own hearts. As far as securing a prescription for effective parenting is concerned, there is no other source that can nearly compare with a personal relationship with God. God made children and no one is better equipped to give instruction or impart wisdom for their proper development than their Creator.

A father recently asked me. "What is the single most important advice you would impart to a father regarding the proper training of his children?" I replied that he must first be an example of what he wants his children to become, plain and simple. It is a general principle that one cannot lead a person further than he himself has travelled. Deuteronomy 6:6–7 admonishes: "These words must first be in thine heart…, and then you should teach them diligently unto thy children." We must first model in our own lives what we want our children to become.

In his book *Guiding Your Family in a Misguided World*, Dr. Tony Evans reiterated the importance of family worship and good communication within the home circle. He states: "Children who have clear moral values taught to them at home will have a much easier road when they're on their own." (Tony Evans, *Guiding Your Family in a Misguided World,* Wheaton, IL: Tyndale House).

Parenting—an Honorable Task

The old adage is still true that the hand that rocks the cradle rules the world. One of my favorite authors, Ellen White, reminds us that the mother who trains her children for Christ is as truly working for God as is the minister in the pulpit. – (PK 219.1) In the government of heaven, parenting is considered to be a work of a high order.

Schools are encouraged to place their most competent teachers at the lowest levels, because the proper training of children requires the expertise that is commensurate with the fragile and sensitive nature of their developing minds. Also, their young minds can be damaged or improved depending on the quality of the instruction they receive at that stage. Childhood is the most important stage of a person's life. "The lessons that the child learns during the first seven years of life have more to do with forming his character than all that it learns in future years" (E. G. White, CG 193.1).

I feel compelled to share with you the following quotes that delineate the importance of early training, not only on the character development of the child, but also on his choice of career:

> Napoleon's Heritage—The character of Napoleon Bonaparte was greatly influenced by his training in childhood. Unwise instructors inspired him with a love for conquest, forming mimic armies and placing him at their head as commander. Here was laid the foundation for his career of strife and bloodshed. Had the same care and effort been directed to making him a good man, imbuing his young heart with the spirit of the Gospel, how widely different might have been his history [13] ("The Signs of the Times," October 11, 1910, CG 196.1).

> Hume and Voltaire—It is said that Hume, the skeptic, was in early life a conscientious believer in the Word of God. Being connected with a debating society, he was appointed to present the arguments in favor of infidelity.

He studied with earnestness and perseverance, and his keen and active mind became imbued with the sophistry of skepticism. Erelong he came to believe its delusive teachings, and his whole afterlife bore the dark impress of infidelity (CG 196.2).

When Voltaire was five years old, he committed to memory an infidel poem, and the pernicious influence was never effaced from his mind. He became one of Satan's most successful agents to lead men away from God. Thousands will rise up in the judgment and charge the ruin of their souls upon the infidel Voltaire (CG 196.3).

By the thoughts and feelings cherished in early years every youth is determining his own life history. Correct, virtuous, manly habits formed in youth will become a part of the character and will usually mark the course of the individual through life. The youth may become vicious or virtuous, as they choose. They may as well be distinguished for true and noble deeds as for great crime and wickedness [14] (Ibid., CG 196.4).

Hannah's Reward—Opportunities of inestimable worth, interests infinitely precious, are committed to every mother. During the first three years of the life of Samuel the prophet, his mother carefully taught him to distinguish between good and evil. By every familiar object surrounding him she sought to lead his thoughts up to the Creator. In fulfillment of her vow to give her son to the Lord, with great self-denial she placed him under the care of Eli the high priest, to be trained for service in the house of God ... His early training led him to choose to maintain his Christian integrity. What a reward was Hannah's! And what an encouragement to faithfulness is her example! [15] (*The Review and Herald*, September 8, 1904, CG 197.1).

Single parents, you may feel that you are alone on this sublime journey, but the God who is a Father to the fatherless, a Mother to the motherless, and a friend that sticks closer than a brother is committed to guide you safely, if you acknowledge His assistance.

> "In all thy ways acknowledge Him, and
> He shall direct thy path" (Proverbs 3:6).

Parenting—a Challenging Task

Single parents face countless challenges on a daily basis. In addition to meeting the daily needs of their children, they grapple with commitment related to work, coupled with other social and emotional pressures, not excluding loneliness, guilt, and a sense of inadequacy.

Studies have consistently confirmed that the majority of single parents are women. These mothers face a unique challenge, especially when they have sons. The lack of a fatherly presence in the home deprives them of a model whereby they can learn, by precept and example, the attributes of real manhood. It is in cases such as this that the church can play a pivotal role in establishing "big brother" programs where the mature men of the church can offer mentorship and guidance to these boys.

Single parents are hereby reminded that regardless of the challenges attendant upon singlehandedly raising your children, you can still make a positive impact. Seek to build a lasting relationship with your children, remembering that closeness now prevents a generation gap later. Teach them to rise at early dawn, and sow in their fertile minds the seeds of God's word before the devil sows his thorn.

It is a truism that if we don't teach our children to love God, the devil will teach them to hate God. Invest in their lives. Empty your purse in their brains by buying them good character-building books. Teach them good values and attitudes, so that as they depart your walls and assume their role in the world, you will stand proud and satisfied that you have prepared them as fit citizens for this world and the world to come.

> It is easier to build strong children
> than to repair broken men.
> —Frederick Douglass

THE JOY OF THE LORD
IS MY STRENGTH.

But they that wait upon the LORD shall
renew their strength; they shall mount
up with wings as eagles; they shall run,
and not be weary; and they shall walk,
and not faint (Isaiah 40:31).

Enjoying the companionship of friends is one way
to enliven and boost your drooping spirit. But you can
relish the experience of a more delightful and enduring
encounter. Excuse yourself from the noise of the crowd
or the din of business engagements. Go alone in a
solitary place. With sincerity of heart and soul hunger,
pray to the One who made you and understands you
more than anyone else:

My loving and eternal Father, I know you love me. I really need you in my heart, in my soul this very moment. Please rid me of everything that's contrary to your will—all sin, all unrighteousness. Remove them far from me. Having cleansed the soul temple, please fill the vacuum with your divine spirit. Bathe my trembling heart, wash me, purge me, purify me, and strengthen me. In Jesus's name. Amen.

Hover o'er me, Holy Spirit,
Bathe my trembling heart and brow;
Fill me with Thy hallowed presence,
Come, oh, come and fill me now.

Refrain:
Fill me now, fill me now,
Holy Spirit, fill me now;
Fill me with Thy hallowed presence,
Come, oh, come, and fill me now.

Cleanse and comfort, wholly save me,
Bathe, oh, bathe my heart and brow;
Thou dost sanctify and seal me,
Thou art sweetly filling now. [Refrain]
Elwood H. Stokes

TIPS TO REMEMBER

**It is better to be a happy single
than a miserable double.**

To all my single friends, before you tie the knot,
please observe a few tips that could save you a lifetime
of misery and unfathomable pain:

1. Listen carefully to the advice and counsel of
   your god-fearing parents. Why? Your father
   knows men; your mother knows women.

2. If you are a teenager contemplating marriage,
   tread softly and carefully. Ask yourself this
   question. Am I mature enough to judge the
   fitness of one to whom I must commit myself for
   the rest of my life? Be sure to seek counseling.

3. Is this person to whom I am about to commit the lifelong guardianship of my affection emotionally and spiritually mature enough to treat me with dignity and to love and cherish me above all others?

4. Has he/she conquered the art of commitment and fidelity, or is he/she still flirting with other members of the opposite sex? Do you still have doubts about his ability to be faithful to you? If the answer is yes, then for the sake of your eternal hope and happiness, don't hesitate to run as fast as you can. If he is unfaithful to you prior to the marriage, expect him to be unfaithful during the marriage.

5. Does he/she already have a dynamic personal relationship with God? If no, then your hope of a happy and spiritually charged marriage is quite dim. The saying is true: "If he does not change to get you, he will not change to keep you." Remember, friends, if you would not eat forbidden fruit, don't venture under the forbidden tree.

6. The reception of the Holy Spirit in the heart means that all other blessings will follow in its

train. In addition to a deep sense of joy and peace, there will be strength of character, a clear definition of our identity, and a true purpose for living. Every single and youth has access to this inestimable gift. Like Pentecost, God will shower the Holy Spirit upon all who earnestly seek Him from a heart of sincerity and soul hunger.

NOTES

Chapter 4

1. J. S. McIlhaney Jr. and F. M. Bush, *Hooked: New Science on How Casual Sex Is Affecting Our Children* (Chicago: Northfield Publishing, 2008). 51, 52

2. Ibid. 40

Chapter 7

Myles Munroe, YouTube video.

Chapter 8

Lynn Toler, *"Divorce Court"*. "Television Show".

Chapter 11

C. Ingram, *Love, Sex and Lasting Relationship* (Grand Rapids, MI: Baker Book House, 2003), 179.

Chapter 13

W. C. Smith, (1865), *One Thing I of the Lord Desire.* https://www.youtube.com/watch?v=MofhksVezgQ

Chapter 17

T. Evans, *Guiding Your Family in a Misguided World.* (Illinois: Tyndale House, 1991), 182.

Chapter 18

1. Case. D, *Bible Studies. David & Bathsheba.* (1997–2012). *http://www.case-studies.com/david4*

2. E. G. White, *Conflict and Courage.* (Hagerstown, MD: Review and Herald Publishing, 2008), 179.

3. Ibid. 181.

4. Case. D, *Bible Studies.David & Bathsheba. http://www.case-studies.com/david4*

Chapter 19

E. H. Stokes, (1879), *Hymnary.org : Hover o'er me, Holy Spirit*—**www.hymnary.org/text/hover over me holy spirit**

Printed in the United States
By Bookmasters